Stay Young
The Golden Years Are the Pits

by

Susan Lancaster

Snosrap Publishing, Nanaimo, BC, Canada

First Published by Snosrap Publishing

3835 Hammond Bay Road,
Nanaimo, B.C. V9T 1G4
Telephone: 250-585-5284

E-mail: sanden39@shaw.ca
http://snosrappublishing.com

Printed in Canada

ISBN 978-0-9730350-4-9

Also by Susan Lancaster

Fiction

The Diamond Talisman

The Caves and The Skull

Hell's Gate

Non-Fiction

The Frog Snogger's Guide

Booklets

80 Practical Ideas to Help You Start a Life
Beyond Self-Doubt

Manners Do Matter

AUTHOR'S NOTE

I offer grateful thanks to Jean Oliver for allowing me to include three of her stories in this book, to Denis Parsons for his contribution about the Dumplings and to Richard Molnar for his assistance in the finalization of the book.

TABLE OF CONTENTS

MUSINGS OF AN OLD BIDDY 1

A MOTLEY COLLECTION OF MUSINGS 7

DOGS AND WILDLIFE 33

SPIRIT 49

FAMILY AND FRIENDS 57

IN THE KITCHEN
AND SLIGHTLY ON THE LARGE SIDE 71

ON THE ROAD AGAIN 85

LOSING IT 97

MUSINGS OF AN OLD BIDDY

SERIOUSLY/FUNNY
MUSINGS OF AN OLD BIDDY

This funny but serious little book reflects on everyday actions we take for granted in our life – or should I say our younger, more productive life. But at times these actions can be plagued by our state of health to the point of frustration as we age.

I know when we are younger, we think, and quite positively too, that we will not really have any problems until the day we die. Therefore, we are ill-prepared when body parts, both physical and mental begin to fall apart or stop working.

Unfortunately there is no age limit for the development of bodily deterioration sent to test us. Sometimes it's early, sometimes it's late and we can't nip into a body parts shop to get replacements or patch ups in just a day or so. But for some of us these aches and pains don't bother us at all.

Stay Young The Golden Years Are the Pits is a collection of jottings and musings of personal happenings and events – both funny and serious and includes animals, trips to various places, touching on God, family and friend's activities, memories in the kitchen, and forgetfulness with lack of focus – tell me about it!

The purpose of this book is two-fold. The book echo's the problems and pitfalls we all meet when growing old. It is definitely an asset if you can keep a positive attitude when dealing with this aging business and the inherent challenges it brings. With this in mind, I try to see the humour in all our circumstances and this may help to lift our spirits, deal with the situation, and get on with our lives without becoming depressed.

The other purpose is to help younger people realize that eventually we do get old, we do have problems, and we must recognize this fact and not push it to the back of our minds and wait for the inevitable to happen. We must accept what life may be like as we age and work to prevent these changes, just by adequately looking after ourselves and our health.

Obviously, some totally unexpected issues will surface, but on the whole we can go a long way to prepare ourselves for continued quality of life through thick and thin as we age.

The characters writing this book are old biddies. Many of you will be asking for the definition of an old biddy. An old biddy is a predominately English term used with a certain amount of mock reverence to describe an older woman. But again, what is old? For the younger person reading the book it may be someone over fifty, but for a woman of fifty, it probably is someone in her eighties such as my mother who said the following about old biddies:

"Oh, I'm not going down to eat with those old biddies," said my mother, in reply to my question about eating plans, "I will have lunch in my room, thank you." Whereupon, she turned back to read her book and that was the end of any further conversation.

They say many a true word is spoken in jest, so I jokingly reminded my Mother that she herself was an old biddy, so why was she complaining about the old biddies downstairs. Obviously, this joke didn't go down well and she flattened me with such a look and frantically started her crossword. I never pursued it any further.

This all took place in a very attractive nursing home amongst the hills of Wales, UK, where my mother spent the last ten years of her life. I live in Canada, and therefore didn't see her as often as I wanted, unfortunately, because she was not only my mother, but also my best friend. Let me tell you I needed her wonderful words of wisdom on many occasions after she'd gone.

Mother was in her mid to late eighties when she started to describe other women as old biddies. In comparison, I'm quite a bit younger, but I've decided the term "old biddy" suits me quite well and allows me to be somewhat acerbic about the older generation, and the younger one for that matter.

Before leaving you, I must mention that three musings in this book were written by one other old biddy, Jean. There is also an article written by Denis, who just felt he should not be left out.

Enjoy the musings of two old biddies and one of the older male of the species.

Reading this book will help you to stay young in mind and body and to be prepared for the Golden Years. If you do that, in your case they won't be The Pits.

A MOTLEY COLLECTION OF MUSINGS

GHOSTS IN THE ATTIC

"What was that?" Denis exclaimed. "Where's Dog?"

"Dog's here, by my feet; what's the problem?"

"Didn't you hear that thud?"

No, I hadn't heard the thud and since Denis didn't seem overly concerned about it, the silent evening continued with us both working away at our respective tasks.

A couple of hours later, there was another thud and I heard it this time. Odd, I thought, the house does creak and groan from time to time as old houses do, but I'd never heard a thud before now. I was just trying to work all this out when there was yet another thud. Not a very loud one, but it definitely sounded as though someone or some object was coming into contact with the wall. The trouble is, the attic only has outside walls and this sounded like an inside thud – not an outside thud.

We experienced this noise later in the evening in what appeared to be in the attic above our bedroom, but we still couldn't figure out what it was. I can't say we were frightened or particularly worried about it, but it was an uncomfortable feeling.

Obviously this thump, once started, didn't feel like stopping and we heard it the following day and again in the evening, whereupon I decreed steps must be taken to investigate. Denis flatly refused to go up into the attic, and I couldn't go up into the attic because of a gammy leg so, working on the assumption it must be some sort of large rodent, or, heaven forbid, even a raccoon, we called our friendly pest control expert the following morning.

Dave arrived just before noon and I was anxious to find out if he had been called out for this kind of thing before.

"Oh, lots of times," said Dave, with a large grin spreading from one ear to the other, "but most of the time it's just ghosts in the attic!" Knowing what my reaction might be to that last sentence, he hurriedly climbed the ladder to the attic.

He found nothing, certainly no raccoon. After he climbed down the ladder, he heard the thud, which prompted him to revise his opinion of ghosts in the attic and he decided to take a tour around the house outside.

Five minutes later, he reported back with his findings. We were all agog thinking that our little mystery might soon be solved.

"It could well be something to do with the attachment of the main electric cable to the house," Dave explained. This power cable swung across the road and up to the side of the house, where it was attached to some kind of fixture on the outside wall.

"Phone Hydro," he suggested.

My heart sank and all I could see were dollar signs and pass-the-buck scenarios with Hydro. B.C. Hydro is the name of the company that supplies all our electrical power.

The following day, having heard more "thumps in the night," I called Hydro. The operator at the other end of the phone explained that the gadget that attaches the cable to the house is called an *emily knob* and as such was not Hydro's responsibility. Ah, I thought, we are running true to form – pass the buck. The operator suggested I call an electrician.

Friday morning dawned, with more thuds during the night, and I was on the phone to the electrician. Yes, they would come out some time today.

Two electricians turned up at one thirty and did a thorough investigation, absolutely intrigued with their unusual problem at this residence. Apparently the *emily knob* was sound and secure, as was the electric cable attached to it. Since the cable entered the house below the attic line, the electricians ruled out the *emily knob* or the cable being the cause of our small problem. Why were Dave, Denis and I not able to figure that out before I called Hydro. I guess because we're not electricians.

While standing at the bottom of the ladder to the attic, both electricians heard the thud, and raced back up again to see what they could see – absolutely nothing. Finally, they left, completely perplexed, as was I. What next, I wondered with a sinking heart as I was beginning to believe ghosts were living in the attic.

What came next was a cessation of thumps and thuds and a huge bill from the electricians, which did nothing but make me rant and swear.

Life settled down and we didn't hear another sound for about three weeks, but then the thudding started again.

While reading my book one evening, I heard a thud and I just couldn't believe it. What was going on? Again, Denis and I toured the house and found nothing that could be the cause of this problem.

After two or three days of this intrusion into our daily lives, we decided something had to be done, but what? Since we couldn't identify the noise, it was difficult to know the qualified person needed to fix the problem. Our best bet, we felt, might be someone in construction because we were now convinced something was going on in the basic roof construction and if it wasn't fixed we had visions of part of the roof collapsing.

The following evening, Denis walked into the lounge with a smug grin on his face and announced he had found "the ghost."

"What?"

"You'll never guess. They are the speakers belonging to my computer."

"But that's in your office, not the attic," I reminded him.

"Come and see," said Denis as he started to walk back to the office.

He twiddled the knob on the speaker and increased the volume. Sure enough we heard the hollow, rather loud static bang that sounds exactly like a thump on the wall in the rest of the house.

Since Denis's office was at the end of the house, I could see how the sound could reverberate and appear to be coming from other places.

"We can easily put this to the test," said Denis, "by turning off the speakers and then putting them on again." Definitely, it was the speakers, and when they were off we never heard another sound. One hundred and fifty five dollars later our problem was solved.

So much for our ghosts! The moral of this story is – if you think you have ghosts in the attic, check the speakers attached to the computer first.

I was telling this story to someone yesterday, and she asked me if I seriously believed in ghosts?

Do you?

REAL OR IMAGINED?

We were looking forward to visiting this old, empty house, Wynnstay, as recommended by the local tourist board. The driveway to the house was long and winding, and periodically we noticed building supplies lying on the edge of the grass, waiting to be used. As the main house came into view, we obviously expected to see signs of new construction or alterations, but there was nothing. This house looked very much the grand country home it had been. We knew it had been empty for years, but it still looked preserved enough that you could expect someone to come or go through the magnificent front door at any time.

We parked the car and admired the gently rolling Welsh countryside that lay beneath the house on three sides. It was quite breathtakingly beautiful and peaceful. My husband wanted to go off on his own to photograph the house, so I set out to walk down to a small lake situated towards the perimeter of the grounds.

As I approached the water, I stopped dead in my tracks. Seated by the side of this small, cheerless lake, was a lady in a cloak with long black hair partially covered by a hood. Her mode of dress was straight out of medieval times! I stared and blinked my eyes hard to ensure that this was reality and not just my imagination. I felt a mixture of fear and anxiety seeping through me. I forced myself to go one step closer to have just one more look.

Slowly, I relaxed a little. Of course, this must be

one of a troupe of actors who visit historical sites to bring various legends to life. I had seen them not long ago at Ruthin Castle all dressed in Elizabethan attire. This medieval maiden before me was an actor, and I was quite excited now about the prospect of talking to her. I quickened my pace, only to feel uneasy again as I drew closer and the roots of my hair began to tingle. Her clothes and long hair didn't move, even though the wind was blowing in strong gusts which had been tugging at my hood. Furthermore, it was cold and her clothing appeared to be soft and flimsy with no protection against the wind. Her cloak remained softly draped around her and not a hair on her head was out of place.

I forced myself to go on but with one more step toward the lake she had gone – disappeared! There was just the lake, the lifeless trees of winter rocking in the wind, the sun and the shadow of clouds rushing through the sky. There was no sign of another human being. Clearly it was all in my imagination, although I was far from convinced.

Disturbed, with butterflies in my stomach, I walked quickly back up the hill, anxious to put as much distance as possible between myself and the lake. I tried to pull myself together before re-joining my husband as I stood outside the main entrance of this solid, but deserted great house. This was a house built for prestige, opulent living perhaps and the enjoyment of family and friends, values so important one hundred and fifty years ago. It was built on top of a hill against a spectacular background of Welsh hills and valleys with no protection from the elements.

I took a final look out across the valley to the opposite hillside. There in the distance was the massive medieval Castle Chirk. It seemed odd, odd that these two buildings faced each other and it almost appeared Wynnstay had been erected as a challenge to the supremacy of the huge fortress that is Chirk, built around seven hundred years before the empty shell behind me. Thinking about Wynnstay and Chirk I suddenly remembered the slim figure in the long flowing medieval robes whom I thought I had seen down by the lake!

I shuddered and decided it must have been my imagination. I think.

NOT ANOTHER BARBECUE!

by Jean Oliver

The other day I was at Canadian Tire with Don, my husband, who wanted to buy a replacement bulb for our security light. I volunteered to wait in the car. That was my first mistake, letting him into Canadian Tire on his own. After all, he is a man, and Canadian Tire has hardware and neat tools (although I could never see anything neat about looking at tools and car stuff – definitely a man thing).

Anyway, after I had almost finished reading the car manual he reappeared, bulb in one hand and a nice looking aluminium suitcase in the other hand.

"Look what I bought," he announced with some satisfaction. "The regular price was forty- nine ninety-five and I got it for only fourteen ninety five." It was a nice set of barbecue tools and accessories but the problem is, we don't have a barbecue.

Our son and his girlfriend came over for the weekend. Don showed them this neat tool set he bought "'for a song." Our son asked him if he was going to buy a barbecue.

"Yes, one day," said Don.

I should mention here that we got rid of our old barbecue many years ago because Don really didn't like barbecuing. Why he suddenly liked the idea again, enough to buy a set of barbecue tools, I wouldn't know.

Perhaps it was the barbecued wieners he kept saying were so good when cooked at the model airplane field. If wieners were what Don had in mind, an hibachi would have worked just as well.

Dan suggested that Don should buy the barbecue now so he could help him get it home. Off they went and, of course, they found another deal. Father and son came home with this humongous barbecue. Bearing in mind just two of us live in this house, we now have this 'thing' with six burners and a hot plate on one side, for boiling the kettle, I suppose. On the other side is a pull up shelf, and a bottle opener. Do they even make bottles any more that aren't screw top? But, hey, just in case they do, Don is ready.

He informed me he would do all the cooking and he even went out and paid full price for a barbecue cookbook. So far we have had two salmon steaks and a couple of pieces of chicken and, of course, zucchinis. Unfortunately, I haven't found any sauce I like, so I made my own barbecue sauce which is excellent; it contains alcohol. I now have many different kinds of spices and so forth because the book says you have to use them. Funny thing, though, Don doesn't like steak and I thought that was what a BBQ was all about.

One last thing. Our old barbecue had a rotisserie on which I used to barbecue roasts, chicken and turkey. This barbecue has a place to put a rotisserie, but we can't find one long enough that will fit from end to end. That's probably why this monstrosity was so cheap. Not to be outdone, Don phoned the manufacturer back east and for one hundred dollars they would send him a rotisserie. This barbecue is definitely not the bargain he thought it was.

There has to be a moral to this story somewhere! Maybe it is "never let your husband shop at Canadian Tire alone!" Ah well, until the next time.

THE GOLDEN YEARS – OH REALLY?

About two years ago I faced the prospect of a hip replacement. Fortunately it was not done, because I lost a few pounds and that made all the difference. However, it did make me think of the future and a subject that dominates our minds as we find ourselves unable to do various things at home, in the garden and out in this wide world of ours – seniors' homes or residences.

It is not all a bed of roses.

The good friend I lunched with is a resident in a seniors' home that offers assisted living. On my first visit to see her I thought I was entering a country mansion. In fact the sooner I could sell my house and move in, the better I thought. Oh, it was wonderful. There was a coffee corner, a shop for items such as milk, juice, an elegant dining room, plenty of lounge space in which to relax, large windows allowing the sun to light up the building, gardens and garden rooms. What more could I ask – and above all, no more cooking and no more trying to figure out what to cook.

My friend, Doreen, has a spacious apartment with a good view that I think she enjoys, but since I see her regularly, I am beginning to realize there is a mental cost to all these efficient services and attractive settings, particularly for her.

Doreen, who is semi-paralyzed, gets care to cover the various things she cannot do, and this care amounts to approximately 1.5 hours per day. The care and services

are reasonable, but the management and billing practices
are totally unreasonable. Fortunately Doreen is still very
much in charge of her life and is considerably younger
than most of the residents. If she sees what she deems to
be an irregularity she will go all out to rectify it, which
she did quite recently. But it was like pulling teeth
because staff like to pass the buck, disclaim responsibility,
not communicate among themselves and provide
inadequate management. On top of this, at the back of
my friend's mind was that she might ultimately pay for
this issue by alienating the people who look after her; a
deterrent for a lesser mortal.

We talked quite a bit about this situation, and both of
us felt it was unfair to a number of residents who were not
quite aware of what was going on and therefore oblivious
to any improprieties. They just go with the flow and pay
their bills. Then there are the residents, who would like
to make a statement, but they are old, they are tired and
they lack the will to put up a fight. Many small problems
can be settled but the larger problems can become
drawn-out sagas and that's when the resident loses heart.
Sometimes there are relatives who are only too happy to
step in and help, but many times there are not and the
resident is on his own.

Then there are the subsidized residents who don't
need to care. They are just happy to have a good roof
over their heads and plenty of comforts. They are totally
unaware of what is going on with management or finance
because they don't have bills to pay at the end of the
month.

I am perhaps painting a somewhat gloomy picture, but
it is not all bad. Living in a seniors' home does allow you
to live out your life in relative peace without the worry

and responsibility of house and home, which can be bad enough at times for the elderly. However, for myself, I will stay in my own place for as long as I can possibly manage it – I hope.

Before ending and as an aside, a friend of mine asked me the other day how I was going to continue getting up and down the stairs in my house (and there are lots of stairs – all fourteen of them) in my current condition of restricted movement. I replied that I'm in training and if worst comes to worst, there is always the chair lift!

STRANGERS AT THE FERRY TERMINAL

Very often we grumble about how uncaring people seem to be. This short story should demonstrate this certainly was not so in my case at the ferry terminal.

To open on a high note: Sometimes something nice happens when you least expect it. I was coming home last week on the ferry from Vancouver to Vancouver Island, and completely forgot Friday was not the day to travel on the ferry (line-ups galore), I raced for the 3:00 p.m. sailing from Horseshoe Bay (Vancouver) to Departure Bay on Vancouver Island. It was full.

Grumbling about the frustration of it all, I drove slowly into a holding area to wait repositioning for the next sailing. Two hours to kill, sitting in the car at the ferry terminal – definitely not my choice. As I was sitting there, I began to have a coughing fit – and I mean a real coughing fit, to the point where I felt I was going to be sick. I had no lozenges, no water, and no candies – nothing that would assuage that miserable needle-like jab at the back of the throat which demanded I cough to get rid of it.

Suddenly the door of the van in front of me opened; I tried to catch the eye of the driver as he got out. No luck. Fortunately it was not long before he re-appeared and I signalled to him. Just as I was getting out of the car to meet him, he was there, and I explained my plight.

"Sorry to bother you," I said, trying to suppress yet another cough, "but do you have any candies or anything to help my cough?"

"Nothing," he replied sympathetically, "but wait a minute, we do have some chocolate-coated almonds – I don't know if those would be any good to you?"

I could have hugged him.

"That will be just fine," I replied with grateful thanks. He returned to the car and came back with the candy bag, out of which I helped myself to three almonds. As he was returning to his car, he was beckoned yet a second time by the driver parked on my right, just ahead of me. Returning to speak to me, he suggested the driver of that car may be able to help me further.

It turned out that driver number two had some orange juice, and he went diving into the trunk of the car to retrieve the juice while I admired the two dogs who occupied the back seat.

"You have saved my day," I said to the driver as he returned with the juice. "Thank you so much."

He was all smiles, I was all smiles, and the driver of car number one was all smiles.

How nice strangers are in your hour of need. I certainly won't forget that incident.

GOLDEN YEARS: THEN AND NOW!

You could have heard a pin drop. It was almost as if everyone was sitting there with bated breath waiting for something to happen. The silence was broken only by the sound of the tea trolley and staff serving tea. Tea-time at this private nursing home was definitely not a time for social interaction. I felt I was among a group of people who seemed to have shut out the world and so had nothing to talk about. To a youngster of sixty like me, it was depressing.

The average age of the residents was about eighty five. These people had changed little since thirty years ago when they retired. Their lives since retirement had been regular, ordered and predictable – a slightly modified version of the calm and tranquillity that started in the Victorian era with unchanging and rigid moral values, spilling over to the beginning of World War II. They didn't have to cope with the traumatic changes that evolved from the 1950s onward, and they were certainly not equipped to do so.

Before retirement, each had his expected role to fulfil. The wives concerned themselves with household matters and being there to support their husbands. The men knew they had to support the family financially and make major decisions; subsequently they had life-long secure jobs with good pensions. The financially secure couple always slowed down after fifty as they had been warned by their parents and their parents before them, "to just take things easy."

Divorce or separation was never discussed as it wasn't an option (unless it was between the rich and the famous). Theirs was a small, compact family with however many children they produced, a variety of in-laws, and of course, grandchildren. The extended family wasn't even invented. Innovations in medical science helped prolong their lives and provide a reasonable quality lifestyle. Microcomputers didn't affect them and entrepreneurs was an unknown word.

From the 1950s onward, huge advancements in science and technology have taken place. The view of our residents toward all of this was one of polite acknowledgment and a display of passing interest while knitting needles clacked together, or they paused to glance up from the latest whodunit. As they were no longer part of the working world they could see no reason to let the inevitable changes affect them. Hopefully, during their lifetime, they would not have to use automatic tellers at the banks!

The most important factor shaping their earlier years was the total disdain for sharing personal troubles with other people – it simply wasn't done. Problems had to be solved or borne by those whom they affected and so we had the proverbial "'stiff upper lip" syndrome. Furthermore, by the time public attitude was encouraging more candour and openness, it was too late for this generation to change.

Conversations were based on topics from the outside world which they learned through the media. When the press evolved from being polite, conservative and considerate into the gutter snipe media it has now become, the residents buried their heads in the sand and ignored it.

It was their offspring who finished school in the early 1960s and had lived with change and now can adapt like a chameleon changing its skin without batting an eyelid. They *always* have something to talk about. Like their parents, did the current generation approaching retirement marry, have 2.4 children and live happily ever after? No, I don't think so; it doesn't work that way anymore!

ALL CHANGE

Women started to work (for a variety of reasons but probably most of them were monetary). At first the housewives and stay-at-home moms frowned and condemned the practice as a break from traditionalism and what was expected. As time went by, the same group that condemned the working practice began to see the financial benefits accrued to a working couple's lifestyle, and they, too, began to think about working.

This trend began to pose problems for the children and the husbands. The children in those days began to be known as 'latch-key kids' because they would often come home to an empty house. They didn't like it, although it did have its advantages and in some cases it promoted early independence. Husbands started to feel neglected while their wives became "super mothers" – having it all and doing it all, but never having any time for him.

This situation led to the inevitable breakdown of the family. Women were adapting more readily to change than men. Suddenly they were now independent, and this opened the flood-gates when they realized they didn't need to be dependent on anyone – least of all a man! The world was their oyster. Instead of the limited careers available in the late 1950s and early 1960s, the choice was now endless. Indeed, they also had an option to work for themselves and make a success of it.

This left the husband, and subsequently men in general completely at sea wondering how to cope and, what is more, wondering who he was and what he was supposed to be. Men had to start over and re-assess every aspect of their previously expected role that had changed so dramatically – a distressing time. Women's Liberation was everywhere; not only was the husband being largely ignored at home, but he suddenly saw women as serious competitors for employment.

Because they were so busy, women started to look to their husbands for assistance in the house so they didn't have to 'do it all' even though initially they thought they could. In this age of enlightenment, the husband saw this situation as enabling a practice of one-upmanship and refused to budge partly because he was not accustomed to doing any kind of household chore and partly because he perhaps, quite rightly felt he had already worked an eight hour day and he deserved a rest in the evenings and on the weekends.

Along came the extended family to add even more pressures to the overloaded husband and wife, to say nothing of the children. Life in itself became a battle of keeping up with the in-laws and out-laws.

In concert with the evolution of the family came breakthroughs in medical science. We managed to more or less eliminate most of the contagious diseases that had plagued us early on in the century, but conversely many people were being struck down with physical and mental illnesses that had never existed. Medical science has played a large part in keeping the aging population relatively fit, healthy and alive. This is having and will continue to have an on-going impact on the lives of both the young and the old because the older population is getting larger and the younger generation is proportionately diminishing.

In the early 1980s we had the advent of microcomputers which revolutionized the way we worked. No longer were jobs secure for long periods of time. A new brand of workers sprang up – entrepreneurs who had been given the golden handshake with large redundancy payments. Entrepreneurs were in abundance, moving at a mile a minute, hoping to hit the jackpot. They wanted to be flying their private jet and clicking their fingers to get something done! Some of them made it: the majority did not.

For the majority who did not, there is plenty of time yet to make that dream come true. All the sons and daughters of the residents who occupied the tea room have now completely adapted to change They can now look forward to a longer, quality life, provided they look after themselves, and there is plenty of time to turn themselves into a celebrity before or after they are eighty! Currently they are not yet willing, ready or able to retire. Does this worry them? Not at all; they have been through all of life's changes and are ready to grapple with many more. As far as they are concerned, there are plenty of opportunities. They have years and years of experience behind them and more importantly, change is just another word.

Contrary to what my dear mother said, "You ought to be slowing down now, dear, you are getting too old to be rushing around." I am up and running to try something new and different and I don't think I will ever stop.

I wonder someday, if they still have nursing homes, if we will be sitting there in due course, with nothing to talk about because we have shut out the rest of the world. I think not. We will be re-organizing the nursing home and the world!

MICHAEL JACKSON

From an Old Biddy's Perspective

When Michael Jackson burst onto the pop music scene in the late 1980s and early 1990s, I could see he and I were not going to get along!

I was then in my forties, and for me, he was way too far out. His music was something I would never listen to, and his eccentricity was beyond belief. The odd song I heard completely by accident, was not particularly the kind of voice I appreciated. I didn't see any of his videos and so was completely unaware of any other talents he had. In fact Michael Jackson was a vague, eccentric personality somewhere out there on the horizon in my life and I didn't want to know about him.

That being said, I didn't like the way the press always had him in our faces, whether we liked it or not. The public was forced to swallow much more of Michael Jackson than perhaps they or he wanted. During his various lawsuits and trials, you were compelled to read at least one paragraph of the proceedings because it was all on the front page, and in most cases filled the front page and rolled over to subsequent pages. In spite of my indifference toward him, I never believed for one moment he was guilty of any of the charges brought against him. In my opinion, these legal sensations were the result of a couple of people who had known the star. They saw an opportunity to capitalize on a tenuous situation and blow it out of all proportion. For them, this was all in the name of money, money, money. How pathetic.

I get rattled about the way the press treats celebrities. It is dreadful. The press can do a lot for us, but they can also calmly destroy people's lives without any care in the world. When someone dies, the media goes on a feeding frenzy and pushes forward any material, good or bad, about the subject and their surrounding circumstances; causing people to buy the paper and therefore earn more money for the press.

We have seen this exact same media nonsense with Diana princess of Wales. The media went mad and have since gone to profound lengths to keep her memory in the news with whatever titbit they can find. Unfortunately they are aided and abetted by a voracious component of the public who don't seem to care what they read as long as it provides them with gossip and something they can get their teeth into. It now looks as though we are going down the same road with Michael Jackson. Everybody is suffering; most of all his three children, the rest of his family, his friends and his fans. Do they want to see their idol smeared with put downs and any grotty innuendo the mass communications systems can find?

As mentioned before, the media does have its positive side, and for me, that was taking a whole television news hour to define what Michael Jackson had meant to his fans. At last I was able to see what everyone was raving about, because I watched his dancing, his singing and clips of his private life and interviews.

I was truly amazed. Here was an extremely multi-talented, versatile person. His voice was excellent, his dancing fabulous and his charisma electric. Looking also at some of the interviews he tolerated about his personal life left me truly disgusted with the media. How gross! In addition to all his talents, he was quite a handsome man despite his efforts to change his face.

It has been alleged he died heavily in debt, and, if that is the case, I don't think his estate will be debt ridden for long. In fact, in death he will probably make more money than when he was alive and financially more than compensate for the come-back we never saw.

I am sad he has gone; sad because he was so young, sad because he left three charming children without a father, and sad because his further contribution to his art will never be.

I finally have a new respect for Michael Jackson – he was superb in all he did. I might buy his videos – if I can find them.

Rest in peace, Michael.

DOGS AND WILDLIFE

BLACK AND BLUE GLADIATORS

Lulu, her muzzle bearing tell-tale signs of extra rich strawberry ice cream, sat in her usual position between the two front seats of the car balanced precariously on the gear-shaft casing. Her lovely beady brown eyes darted expectantly between Mother and Granny, hoping more ice-cream was coming her way. She was a beautiful, if somewhat podgy Doberman Pinscher with her black coat glistening in the sunlight. She was enjoying her treat after a long run on the beach and a swim in the sea – a feast of ice cream at the local cafe car park, generously offered by her doting owner and owner's mother (Granny).

Reluctantly she noted that preparations were being made to leave and therefore ice cream-gorging had ended for the afternoon. She settled herself comfortably on her towel on the back seat of the car ready for the journey home. It was a hot day, so all the windows were open allowing a breeze, although not cool, to circulate around Lulu and humans as the car moved off.

Shortly the car drew up at traffic lights, adjacent to a market stall. Between the market stall and the car stood a rather nervous-looking older lady clutching her bicycle, waiting for the lights to change to green. Mother and Granny promptly christened her 'Nervous Nelly'.

Suddenly there was a high pitched yelp from Lulu as she leapt onto a startled Granny's lap with a thud. This abrupt action unleashed a whole chain of unexpected events. Overcome with shock on hearing the yelp,

Nervous Nelly nearly jumped out of her skin momentarily releasing her bicycle which fell over onto the nearest market stall loaded with oranges.

While Mother was trying to calm Granny and dog, there was an angry shout as a precariously balanced crate of oranges, dislodged by the falling bicycle smashed onto the pavement. Oranges cascaded out of the crate and rolled all over the street.

Two volunteers from the crowd gathering to see what was going on went to help the owner of the stall collect the oranges. Unfortunately one of the volunteers stood on an orange which split and he slipped. He put his hand out to grab the nearest thing to steady him which was a hosepipe used to produce a gentle spray to refresh the produce. As he grabbed the hose it was wrenched out of the socket in the wall and the water, which had been carefully controlled in a slow steady trickle for the purpose of watering, now gushed onto the assembled crowd.

As Mother glanced out of the corner of her eye and saw the mounting chaos in the square, the traffic lights turned to green and she decided discretion was the better part of valour as she moved her foot onto the accelerator. She didn't want to be around to witness the next turn of events.

When they arrived home, Mother was determined to find out what made Lulu jump into Granny's lap. She didn't have far to look. There, on the back window ledge of the car was a large, exhausted bluebottle fly in its death throes. She knew only too well that if Lulu encountered a fly the worst was to be anticipated. Given freedom of space, the dog would beat a hasty retreat from the vicinity of the wretched fly – she just couldn't stand them. Any encounter between dog and fly encouraged human involvement to dispatch the fly at the earliest opportunity – a bit difficult in the confined space of a car.

The people in the market square thought they had problems being soaked to the skin and picking up oranges. They just didn't know how lucky they were that Lulu's preference was to jump on Granny's lap instead of out of the window!

PROGRESS (OR OTHERWISE)
OF A FLY-FISHERMAN

A fly-fisherman is a true artist. He casts and performs a beautiful display of loops and curves with his line as he sends it spinning over the water, eventually placing the fly at the end of the line in front of the fish lurking just below the surface; the fish doesn't stand a chance. For the fish it is fatal temptation, and it is not too long before our artist and hero is bringing in the big one (all twelve inches of it)! What poetry in motion, what a feeling of satisfaction, what a tale for the telling.

These thoughts were not exactly in Denis's mind when, in the early 1980s he thought he would try his hand at fly fishing. The nearest river was out of bounds so he spent hours of practicing in a field and even more hours untangling the line from the bush behind him. As he practiced, he dared to think of the triumphs that would be his – perhaps in the not-too-distant future.

Unfortunately, due to a busy workload and lots of other problems that beset our hero, it was not until six years later after arriving in British Columbia, Canada, that he dared to dream again.

Denis was sensing this fly fishing business was not going to be a piece of cake. Weighed down by all kinds of equipment he didn't need as a beginner, he joined the "experts" at two local lakes in Victoria. To his horror his casting had deteriorated, he was using the wrong type of flies and worse still, he created too much of a splash on the lake, immediately advertising his presence to the fish and irritating other anglers nearby.

After a few weeks of getting nowhere, he got fed up and decided on a bit of an excursion into sea fishing. With Michael, his stepson, and Brian, the next-door neighbour, he spent many happy but not so fruitful hours, trolling and spinning for salmon in the Strait of Juan de Fuca.

As he became more practiced in his art, our intrepid hero had to suffer the indignities of overturned canoes, soaked clothes, flies in the hair, stalled engines on the boat, tangled lines and countless other stories to explain 'The one that got away'.

Like so many other amateurs wanting to reach the height of perfection, a never-ending cash flow was required to purchase the "vital" equipment needed to assure success. This included rods – not just any rod but the best hand-made rod of baron/graphite, a descendant of the bamboo rod used in fly-fishing because of its light weight and flexibility. Naturally there was an array of back-up rods designed according to the species of fish to be caught.

Of course, there was the reel to go on the rod. Reels on fly rods are for carrying the fishing line and that is all as far as the layman is concerned. But as with all other fishing equipment, reels come in a variety of sizes for various purposes. Clearly nothing but the best of each type would be appropriate for Denis.

Hooks and flies – without which it is difficult to catch a fish – were added to the ever- swelling inventory. Hooks vary in size, again depending on the type and size of fish being pursued. Prior to the acceptance of the environmental footprint, barbed hooks were used, giving the fish little or no chance of survival. From the writer's point of view, this was particularly cruel when it came to trying to remove them from the fish because the barb was almost impossible to remove without tearing the flesh. Now barb-less hooks are encouraged and indeed, in many places, they are the only hooks allowed. These provide a sporting chance for the fish to 'un-hook' itself as it jumps out of the water and also the hook is easily removed without harm if the fish is to be released back into the water.

Flies – a fly, is a fly, is a fly. Not so when it comes to flies for sports fishing. They come in a beautiful array of colours for all kinds of fish and all kind of weather as well as wet or dry flies. The dry flies float on top of the surface and the wet fly (lure) swims on the surface water or below. In both cases the choice depends on what type of fish the fisherman is chasing, its feeding habits, the environment and the weather.

Having spent a small fortune on equipment so far, it was something of a surprise when our expert decided to tie his own flies. Now, fly-tying was the all-consuming hobby when he was not fishing, and it was much less expensive than buying flies.

Clothing was not exempt from the "'I definitely need" list. When he started fishing, Denis was content with the basics which included a good pair of stout shoes or gum boots. As he progressed in his art, he found waders were a definite asset enabling him to go into the river (hip or chest waders being available). His forays into the river also necessitated a wading stick to test the depth of the waters and the bottom of the river (mud has a habit of sinking).

It was not too long before he realized it was easier to

deal with a broken line or tippet in mid-stream, rather than returning to the river bank to look for the necessary implements and materials to mend the break. Therefore, a fishing vest had to be purchased; otherwise it would be impossible to fish!

A fishing vest is a waistcoat composed of a multitude of pockets upon pockets to hold all the tools of the trade and a variety of clips on which to hang the implements not suitable for pocket storage. Amongst other things, the vest may sport pliers, penknives, files, flies, fly boxes, a thermometer, a flotant, scissors, a fly drying patch and so forth. In fact a well-equipped fly vest, fully loaded, succeeds in presenting our intrepid fisherman as a Christmas tree without lights.

As he climbed the expensive ladder of success to fishing competency and in some cases, outstanding flashes of brilliance, Denis had one important lesson to learn – times of the day and weather. The optimum times for fishing would appear to be between eleven in the morning and two in the afternoon, and one hour before dusk to half an hour after dusk. There are, of course, other times to be tried – all day long if necessary, but those are the times yielding the best results.

As in countless situations other than fishing, the weather is crucial. Equipment and knowledge is required to support each weather condition. A strong cold wind can cause the fish to go deeper into the water. Bright days with a cloudless sky or white clouds tend to enhance the vision of the fish. The ideal condition may well be the still, dull warm day in excess of fifty degrees Fahrenheit. Fish will not rise if the outside air temperature is colder than the water.

Finally, what does our hero see in this sport of fly-fishing? To the layman or onlooker it is a dull, boring, slow and often futile sport, to say nothing of the cost which does not stop at equipment. To fish the rivers can be exorbitantly expensive in fees, unless you are on special waters used by fishing clubs.

As Denis points out, it is the enjoyment of pitting his wits against those of the fish. What wits does a fish have, I ask? He maintains he doesn't have time to think about other mundane problems, and he gets plenty of aerobic exercise, climbing, walking and casting. Above all there is the solitude, the river or lake, the countryside, and the communion with nature. Then there is always the anticipation of catching 'the big one' or just 'a fish' to show for being out all day and half the night!

SAMI

The dog that lay looking at me from out of the monitor window on the internet was nothing less than gorgeous – and she was a poodle: a standard French poodle.

We are dog people and many dogs had gone through our lives, bringing lots of love and companionship to us in every case. We've missed this and decided to get one more dog. Narrowing the field, we began to focus on finding a poodle for several reasons, mainly that it was a non-shed, intelligent anima. We would regret the second criterion very much – from the first day of ownership onwards! The fact that we would one day be interested in owning a poodle was farcical indeed.

After deciding on the breed, I left it to my partner to find a suitable poodle and now I was looking at her on the Internet. She needed a home and that was the start of a love affair between Sami and us. Without hesitation Joe made arrangements to pick her up and bring her across to the Island. I went out to the ferry terminal to meet them, and she was even more gorgeous than I remembered. Cream in colour, she had a long snout and two of the loveliest hazel eyes possible. She was well behaved, rather sedate in a way, and compliant as we put her in the car and drove back to Nanaimo!

She was seven months old and had been through three homes;, we were the fourth. First there was the puppy home and, upon separation from her mother, she was sold to a couple who went to work all day long. This resulted in a partially demolished house by little sharp dog teeth from a pup who objected to being left alone all day long – she had to go. The next home was a family with lots of children, who went bananas over her to begin with, but then, as is usual, the children's promise to look after the dog dwindled away, and she was up for sale again!

This time she went to the owner who sold her to us and who also had another dog. She drove Sami from Abbotsford to the ferry terminal and we gather Sami had to go because the two dogs didn't get along; at least, that's what she said, (I suspect Sami wanted too much attention). Joe mentioned that after he had paid for her and led her away onto the ferry, Sami never even looked back at her previous owner. There was obviously no love lost there.

We were upset that Sami was in three different homes before she came to us and we were eager to give this pup all the love she needed.

In the first week our repayment for this love was forty dollars worth of shoe repair, two antique chair legs chewed at the base, and odd potty accidents but not a huge issue, and she did manage to sleep through the night. After having her for about five days, we took her shopping to be honoured with poop all over the inside of the car because she was left and obviously experienced separation anxiety.

The kitchen was a no-no because she got up on her hind legs and surfed around the counters for food, which, when discovered, mysteriously disappeared. We lost a few expensive cuts of meat. She became a master at picking the sugar bowl up from the table, carrying it in her mouth to the dining room, putting it on the floor, and licking the sugar out of it – all without spilling a drop! It became quite evident we were being trained by Sami. The look in her eyes simply underlined that this was her forever-after home and she wasn't going anywhere. There will, no doubt, be some more news about our training by this JD (juvenile delinquent) dog.

COMMON SENSE

One morning as I was getting ready for the day, I heard the following story on the radio and it made me mad. The gist of the story was about a baby deer found near the dead body of its mother outside a town in British Colombia five years ago. Jill adopted the baby deer and raised it as a pet. Bimbo and Jill became firm friends over the years.

Suddenly, out of the blue, along comes the ministry of the environment; not one month, or one year after this adoption occurred, but five years later, and decrees that the deer must be returned to the wild! Where, oh where is common sense?

I have to agree with the ministry that wild animals should not be kept as pets, but I have to ask what it has done in the past with real wild animals, who pose a huge danger to people if they escape, lions, tigers and snakes, particularly pythons smuggled into the province and kept in cages as pets.

Why did the government not intervene five years ago? I suspect because they didn't know anything about the situation. It had come to light through tales of a pious know-it-all neighbour or individual, or possibly one of these rabid environmentalists who cannot make any kind of exception to any rule.

I am outraged on a number of fronts, not the least of which is severing the bond between animal and human that has been forged over the years. I doubt Bimbo could ever be rehabilitated and returning her to the wild would be returning her to an environment fraught with dangers for her. She is absolutely no threat to the general public and I agree with Jill that the separation of deer and human is not an option. The damage, such as it is, has been done, and the ministry should now butt out and leave the matter well alone.

SPIRIT

A WONDERFUL WOMAN

I need to write about Pat's memorial service because it was different. It wasn't your usual run-of-the-mill solemn, tearful funeral service. It was uplifting, joyous, and a true celebration of a life.

The church was full. Ten minutes to wait before the family arrived. The service began with "All Things Bright and Beautiful", setting the tone for an uplifting occasion. This was a hymn my mother requested to be sung at her funeral, but because my sisters organized everything overseas and I forgot to mention her request it didn't happen. So I sang "All Things Bright and Beautiful" for my mother at Pat's service.

As we moved on after the psalm and readings, a time of remembrance' was recalled by Lisa, Pat's daughter. I knew Pat only as a person I saw once a week in church. We enjoyed a couple of serious conversations, shared grandchildren pictures and occasionally worked church duties together. We had fun. She was a very pleasant person to be around – and she always had the most gorgeous outfits.

Lisa spoke so eloquently about her mother's life. Pat's achievements in her busy life were amazing, and I regretted I had not known her a little better.

We sang "'She Flies On" and the Prayer of St. Francis', both of which highlighted the personality that was Pat.

Our minister shared his talk prefaced by remarks that

Pat, herself, had planned this service. With a wry smile he related how Pat had warned him this gathering was to be a joyous, positive occasion and experience, which it certainly was.

Throughout the service, thoughts came to me periodically. Thoughts about life and death, living, family and marriage and so forth. Pat and her husband Eric had been married for forty five years. Where, oh where is that ethic now? What, I wonder, could have been achieved in society as a whole with many more people in a solid, firm permanent marriage, rather than with second partners and extended scattered families?

Upon concluding the service, Kevin announced Pat was going to have the last word with a recording of "What a Beautiful World" sung by Louis Armstrong. As the strains of this lovely melody and the gravelly tones of Louis Armstrong enveloped the church, all was silent and still. It was almost as if there was a huge communal hug going on between Pat, her family, and friends.

Indeed, I felt Pat was really and truly with us through the entire service, a smile of joy and satisfaction spreading across her face as Louis Armstrong came to the end of his famous song.

May the Lord keep you with Him for all eternity, Pat. We will meet again at some time, some day.

DO YOU HAVE A LIFE PLAN?

The following is an excerpt from a booklet written about changing a poor self-image. We, as old biddies, probably made up our mind a long time ago about the issues discussed in this booklet. I was asked to talk about this booklet to a gathering of about forty-five seniors and was extremely apprehensive because seniors were not my target audience. Surprisingly, afterward everyone bought a copy of the booklet. They didn't want it for themselves; they wanted it for their children and grandchildren.

Whether we admit it or not, the one part of our life that has a profound influence on the way we think is our belief system. Take a few minutes to consider the following before flatly refusing to acknowledge that anyone, other than yourself, is responsible for your destiny.

Decide if you believe (we're not talking other people here, we are talking you), you hold the key to your own destiny and peace of mind, or if God does.

Think about the enormity of that choice because it will affect every facet of your life in the future.

Ask yourself if you have a personal code of ethics to guide you along the way because you will need that, if you decide go it alone. This code might have headings such as "personal conduct", "accountability", "commitment", for example.

Ask yourself about the future and how you are going to conduct it by yourself. Think carefully. It is an awesome undertaking to be totally responsible for yourself for the rest of your life.

Determine if you are going to make yourself the person around whom your world revolves. Will you be the person who makes all the decisions, calls all the shots, and expects everything to fall into place immediately?

Decide if you will be forever seeking material things that you believe will bring you happiness and satisfaction, or if there is another choice?

Resolve also if skills and knowledge, to the exclusion of all else, are going to provide you with the contentment you are seeking.

The above is just part of the subject areas that affect our lives.

There is the other side to beliefs. Maybe it's time to ask God to take responsibility for our lives.

DON'T MESS WITH GOD

Recently the opening of the British Columbia Legislature took place. Prior to the official opening, there was a brief time of prayer for the government and the work it set for itself for the coming session.

I was listening to the local radio station. The topic under discussion by a small panel was the appropriateness of opening the legislature with a brief time of prayer? The following day the comments poured in.

"This kind of thing should never be allowed". "Was it warranted?" "I thought it was rather pleasant", and on and on. All those for and against weighed in.

As I was listening to the pros and the cons, I realized this practice had probably been used at every opening of the legislature for a number of years. This point was borne out later by a guest the following day who confirmed that opening with a prayer has been the tradition since the first legislature sat in British Columbia. I was asking myself why the appropriateness of the practice should suddenly be questioned now.

If the legislature feels it must appeal to a higher power to guide its path in government decisions and policies, then so be it.

Listener replies were many and varied, the main question being the necessity of separating church and state. A visiting professor from Trinity Western University assured listeners there was no constitutional law or legal requirement in Canada to separate church and state. That prerogative, if applicable, was left to our neighbours in the south.

There was also the remark that we all prayed to the same God, who not only listens to prayers as rendered at the opening of the session, but also sanctions suicide attacks on innocent people. The professor hastened to assure us that the latter was not the God of his faith.

Surely the above is all perception – a faith or collective peoples' opinion of what their God would have them do, not necessarily what their God wants them to do.

What was intoned in prayer to God on Wednesday was something that we all hope for anyway, so what is the point of questioning the practice?

Benjamin Disraeli once said, "Never complain and never explain". What a fantastic piece of advice for all of us.

As the learned professor said, there should be no marginalizing of different faiths. What I say is that we should get on with the business of non-condemnation for those who hold different ideas from the ones we hold. Whether atheist, agnostic, Christian, Jew, Hindu, Muslim, Buddhist, and with all due deference to the many other faiths not mentioned, respect other people's views and religions, go about your own business, but don't mess with God.

FAMILY AND FRIENDS

GREAT ADVICE FOR REJECTED WRITERS

Two years ago or so, we saw Susan Boyle, a homely forty-seven-year-old single lady who had a burning ambition to be a professional singer, step onto the world stage with the song, "I Dreamed a Dream," from *Les Miserables*. Now she is the talk of the planet, literally.

What is so special about Susan Boyle? Obviously she has an enormous amount of talent and she also possesses a thick skin thereby ensuring that negative remarks and put-downs could not derail her from her ambition. I thought it was amazing that she could stand there, as bold as brass, on centre stage, with all that jeering and face pulling, and not show any signs of nervousness.

There is no doubt that people find success in life because they have developed the ability to ignore criticism and continue on course until they meet their objectives.

It is easy to say, "Don't let rejection get to you," but it does. You spend months and possibly years nursing this pet project along and finally at the point of presentation the one who makes decisions says no.

It is indeed odd that many people who are gifted and talented do not rise to the heights or even to a modicum of success in life simply because they cannot tolerate rejection. On the other hand, there are other people who are extremely successful with average talent only because they have developed a thick skin and any negative remarks just don't make any impression.

It takes a certain and special type of person to face rejection on a constant basis, thinking particularly of sales personnel and many others exposed to the whim of the fickle Joe Public on a daily basis. We, as authors, (but it applies to everyone) fall into the sales personnel category although, of course, we would never think of ourselves as such. But, my dear colleagues, that is precisely what we are. So, if there are potential authors out there who want to earn some kind of livelihood from writing, please take note of the above, because the books don't walk to the bookstore shelves by themselves.

It is during this time, or even during the writing of the book, that rejection is going to rear its ugly head and we hear that small, two lettered word "no" and the countless reasons to support that decision.

So, what are we going to do about it? It is easy for others to say "Don't let it get to you," but it does, and it hurts. You've spent months and possibly years nursing this baby along and suddenly one bookstore owner says 'no'. Oh, the devastation – it's the end of the world – why, oh why, oh why? What's the point of hanging in there – woe is me!

Is it as bad as that? No, it certainly isn't. After all, the bookseller hasn't read your book which is a masterpiece. Well, then it's his loss, so let's try the next one. But before going on to the next one, make sure you know why that particular person didn't want to carry your book and learn from the reply.

We must recognize that the primary tool for fighting rejection is our own attitude. An example of this is Beryl, who is a writer. After her book had been printed, faults were found that made the book unsalable. If I'd have been Beryl, I'd have stamped my foot, screamed with rage, blamed everyone but me, thrown out all the books and then made a vow never to write again. What did Beryl do? She believed in the book, fretted, wept and then decided to fix the problem and get that book on the market. It taught her a valuable lesson but she didn't give up although she had every right so to do.

What do we do when doors seem to close on us and we take it oh, so personally?

This sounds negative, but don't anticipate people are going to say yes. Pray for yes, cross your fingers for yes, but never anticipate yes. There is a huge difference – when you don't expect it and don't get it, then the disappointment is not quite so bad.

If you receive a no – you must realize this is only one person's point of view. Don't take it to heart. You know your book will ultimately more than pay for itself so just move on.

Uncovering the reason for rejection often helps determine future policy and eliminates disappointment on your part.

Susan Boyle waited forty seven years for success. Go for it and get that masterpiece on the market. Good luck!

ONIONS AND CARROTS GALORE

I had the pleasure of talking recently with my step-son in the UK. He is quite a guy, a person able to make goals and stick to them in the face of adversity. Iain and his wife, Suzanne, recently moved into another house that requires a lot of tender loving care and a lot of money that goes automatically with TLC. Suzanne is a great decorator and I know when the house is finished, it will look superb.

They also acquired an acre of land with the house, with two dog runs dominating the landscape. The previous owner, I understand, was a dog breeder. With a mind to cut the cost of living, which is prohibitively high in England, Iain and Suzanne decided to turn one of the dog runs into a sort of allotment plot. In the middle of house renovations, and work, Iain made the decision to rent a rotovator and transform the one dog run into a viable piece of land on which to grow veggies of all sorts, sizes, and descriptions.

Iain, being Iain, had done all his market garden research thoroughly before committing to this plan, including price comparisons with what was available in the supermarket and the best growing facilities for the produce. He discovered that in some cases, buckets will work! I was getting so enthused with his descriptions, I pictured myself running out to buy buckets to grow various vegetables on the deck – mmm, fresh.

He announced he had bought three packets of carrot

and onion seeds, hoping it would be enough. When he arrived home and looked closely, at the packets, he discovered one packet of carrot seeds would produce 3,500 carrots, and one packet of onion seeds would produce 2,600 onions. He decided to refrain from purchasing any more carrot and onion seeds.

I could not restrain my laughter and suggested that perhaps he'd better set up a vegetable stall outside the house, which would contribute further to his increased economic status.

Finally our phone call came to an end, and I immediately went to see my husband and suggested we should resurrect the appropriate pots and frames to grow tomatoes and peppers on the deck. With an uncertain economic future, maybe we should be using common sense and producing fresh, organic vegetables for ourselves. It made sense, and, after all, there is nothing like home grown tomatoes.

THE SKYTRAIN

The Skytrain is a network of overhead railways that link all places in Vancouver, British Columbia, Canada, and this story just goes to prove how ignorant and positively stupid I was to venture via this method of transportation at ten o'clock on a Saturday night to downtown Vancouver.

I had been working non-stop packing and cleaning at the condominium and decided to call it a day at about ten o'clock. My son called me from downtown and offered to come and collect me from Burnaby in the car. I assured him there was no problem and he could pick me up at Burrard Station in downtown Vancouver.

Off I went with friend Bob, who drove me to the Metro station, and I boarded the Skytrain after just a few minutes' wait. Settling myself down in the middle coach, to the rear, I took out some reading material (don't even remember what it was).

At the following station a couple of men boarded the train. One was tallish, a little on the chubby side, with a round face and totally out of it – drunk as a lord. The other man was much quieter but seemed prepared to follow up on any remarks that came non-stop from his friend.

When they stepped onto the train, the first thing the drunken lord shouted was "Well, there's Grandma and how's Grandma this evening?" I nearly died, but I am not sure whether it was because of fear or outrage. Outrage that apparently I looked my age – how dare they! Hadn't I been told dozens of times that I didn't look my age? The quieter individual made his way to behind my seat and sat down to peer over my shoulder to see what I was reading, while there was a stream of unending grandma remarks coming from the drunken lord, who had parked himself, thank goodness, by the door. There were no abusive remarks uttered, but I slowly started to get quite concerned because I was not sure where it all would end.

I sat rigidly staring at my book, not giving them the satisfaction of even recognizing the grandma tirade, and I could see the three young girls in front of me showing a bit of concern.

Having received no joy in getting any reaction from me, the two men suddenly disappeared to the other end of the car, and started on another subject targeting other passengers with a stream of non-ending remarks. I relaxed a little, but not for long, because they soon came back and started on about grandma again. All of a sudden, one of the young girls sitting in front of me let him have it.

"For f------........ sake why don't you just shut up?" she yelled at the top of her voice. "Leave her alone," (Grandma, that is.)

Just as she was about to hurl further rage in his direction -- and I think, if necessary, get up and hit him -- we drew up at a station, the doors opened and there was a couple of Skytrain policemen. Never was I or everyone else in that car so thankful as they yanked the drunken lord out of the car onto the station platform.

The young girls in front of me immediately turned to make sure I was OK, and I assured them with a forced smile that I was a tough old bird and would survive. They were not to know I had a heavy handbag at the ready at

all times, and would have lashed out with all my strength
if the drunken lord and his mate had approached me
physically.

We concluded that unbeknownst to us, someone at
the other end of the car must have called for help and
there was definitely a communal sigh of relief when the
closing doors shut out our intruder.

What a journey. Obviously I had been living in
the past and had expected the journey to be calm and
uneventful. Fat chance!

WHO IS THE BABY-SITTER?

Although our children would dearly love us to baby sit their children it can be a practice fraught with dangerous possibilities – read on.

I was chatting on the phone the other day to my ex-husband in Vancouver about our granddaughter. Having just returned from Asia recently, my son, daughter-in-law, and granddaughter Vera, then age four, were staying with Grandpa for a short while.

My son and his wife didn't go out often, but they did like to get away to do some grocery shopping for a couple of hours without Vera tagging along.

Grandpa was not happy about this because he was the one left to babysit. It is not that he doesn't like looking after Vera, but the problem is he has a habit of nodding off throughout the day and doesn't feel he is a responsible baby-sitter any more. In fact, it worried him that he wasn't able to look after his beloved Vera to the best of his ability.

Grandpa decided that this practice of baby-sitting had to stop; a decision that weighed heavily after my son took a recent half hour trip to the store, leaving Vera with Grandpa. As our son was going out of the door he turned back and reminded Vera she had to keep an eye on Grandpa and make sure he didn't go to sleep. If he did go to sleep, then she must wake him up. Vera responded she was quite capable of looking after her Grandpa.

Who, is minding whom, I ask?

THE SHOPPING EXPEDITION

If there are two items on a shopping list, I always thought it would take about half an hour to do the shopping. Not so, as the years move on and especially not if the trip involves a husband. Today, as well as the two things, we needed at the grocery store we had to stop at the bank to sign a form, which would probably take a couple of minutes. Anything involving Denis immediately places the expedition in danger, so we need a half-hour (or longer) planning session to figure out where we are going and what we are going to do. In fact the entire operation makes planning for a trek to the Himalayas looks like child's play.

Naturally the dog had to come too, since Rufus refuses to accept the term "guard the house". The first call, the bank, went smoothly and when we returned to the car, I mentioned to Denis that the next stop was Fabricland for me to get a zip. I also explained he would wait in the car while I purchased said zip, and then I would take the dog and walk to Superstore about half a kilometre from Fabricland, while he went by car to pick up some gas. I shouldn't even have mentioned this plan as it took the whole of the car journey for Denis to understand what was going to happen when we left Fabricland.

Zip was purchased, I collected the dog from the car and off we went on our separate ways. I walked to the front of Superstore by the disabled parking lots, but was beaten by Denis, who not only swooped into a spare parking lot, but promptly reversed with great precision and went back the way he had come – at great speed, I might add. As he was executing this tricky bit of driving, I heard the following:

"I paid for the gas," he called from the car window, "but forgot to put the gas in the car – won't be long." Rufus and I stood there with our mouths hanging open – had it really come to this?

When Denis arrived back at the gas pump, there was a car occupying the space by his pump, but of course the pump wouldn't start because Denis hadn't used it. Upon arriving in the office, the attendant told him she saw him leave without filling the car and immediately turned the pump off. So, it fell to Denis to explain to the two people who were in a state of exasperation at the pump not working, that they had to move to another pump so he could fill his car with the gas he forgot to put in on his first trip! I didn't even want to know about the reaction of the waiting couple.

Finally he returned with a full tank of gas and we managed to shop without further incident, except I couldn't get the prescription I wanted, and we had to go to another store.

It was there, while waiting for the prescription to be filled, that I sat talking to the ninety year old, who, in my estimation, looked seventy. She had quietly been waiting for at least twenty minutes for someone to give her some information. We commiserated about how long it took to do something these days, even if it was just waiting for information. She was also complaining about the fact that every time she saw her son-in-law, he was on her case about what she should eat or not eat, plus the fact that she should come off all medication. She retorted on each occasion that obviously she was eating the right thing because she had reached the age of 90 and she saw no necessity to change. Brilliant.

As we entered the parking lot of the next pit stop Denis suddenly started to drill me about the Stilton cheese.

"Did you get the Stilton cheese at Superstore?" he asked.

"No," I said, " I thought you were going to do that."

"No, I forgot to do it, would you buy some Stilton in Thrifty's?"

And so it goes on. What should have been a half-hour shopping trip, turned into a whole morning's nightmare.

IN THE KITCHEN
AND SLIGHTLY ON THE LARGE SIDE

WALKING TENT

As we grow older, there is a tendency to shrug off any concerns of the past about how we look and how we feel. Many of us have reconciled ourselves, either consciously or subconsciously, to the state of "what you see is what you get," and we simply don't worry any more. On the other hand, there are people who do care how they look and how they feel, but they hide this concern very well.

Speaking for myself, I am definitely of the "what you see is what you get," variety except for one thing – weight. When I retired I was delighted to assume the mantle of the Walking Tent. For me, the incentive to be a specimen of the perfect woman disappeared immediately when I no longer had to go out to work.

So, I now get up in the morning and throw on the Walking Tent, a loose garment that hides a multitude of sins, or a pair of jeans and top two sizes too big for me, which fools me into thinking I've lost weight, a feeling that persists until I get on the scales – and then all hell breaks out.

Make-up, what's that? I'd almost forgotten to mention it. Who is left to impress? I think my husband regards me as part of the furniture, so I don't invest in the effort to "tart" myself up – who cares?

Being on the latter side of sixty tends to encourage us to cocoon, perhaps even more so if the scales are governing our lives. If, because of our somewhat large frames, we suffer from pangs of negative self-confidence, remaining at home provides us with a marvellous reason to enjoy our solitude and become thoroughly antisocial.

Perhaps in the end, we tend to view our physical selves as something resembling bean bags, or soufflés on the verge of collapse. We make sure the number of mirrors in the house are receding in size and quantity, but are grateful that our bodies continue to serve us well. Some of us take an occasional peek into the remaining mirror and have seen the drooping boobs, the wrinkled face, and the sagging muscles on various parts of ourselves. We see and accept these facts, but we don't worry about them because why should we? No matter what anyone will tell you, we still feel the same as we felt in our twenties, but at least we accept the bikini days are long past worrying about.

The other side of the argument is that we should care – for a variety of reasons; most of all because being overweight can cause severe problems in the later years. Caring about ourselves engenders an interest in caring about other people. Caring about other people prohibits us from becoming selfish and antisocial. Caring what we look like gives us confidence in ourselves and maybe a new interest in improving our ho-hum routine. But, possibly I just can't be bothered; you get like that, you know.

HOW TO CLEAN A TURKEY

Since I am no great cook, I don't write much about food, but I feel prompted to tell you about my not-so-yummy experiences with a Christmas turkey because cooking this turkey revealed something unknown to me.

Following the collection of the ten-pound bird from the store, we kept it cool in the fridge for two days before Christmas. After completing the necessary preparations before cooking we put it in the oven on Christmas Day to cook according to the instructions on the plastic cover of the bird.

Removing it from the oven after the appropriate amount of cooking time, it seemed a little on the tough side and my husband felt that it needed another half hour. We gave it another half hour, and it was still a bit on the tough side but we decided to eat it anyway.

I think *that* Christmas was the first time I didn't enjoy my turkey – it was tough. It certainly didn't have a succulent turkey flavour and we had no idea why.

Neither one of us wanted to have cold turkey the following day, so the next best thing was to boil it all up and make a soup. What a mistake! An awful smell pervaded the kitchen, and I couldn't figure out what it was. It was a smell I had experienced once before with some turkey legs cooked for the dog. For want of a better description, I detected a definite smell of stale bleach. Before I finished cooking the soup, the entire content was thrown out and that was the end of our turkey.

A few days later I was in the store that supplied us with the turkey, and I felt, after some indecision I had to mention the turkey, and I did. The meat manager was most sympathetic and was glad I reported it. He would get in touch with the suppliers.

A week later the suppliers were in touch with us, and admitted to my husband that just before they are finally packaged, the birds are bleached and rinsed, and occasionally one slips through the rinsing stage. In our case, the bird that missed the rinsing stage was our turkey!

We were reimbursed by the company but to me it was one more nail in the coffin of processing food. Yuk!

FAT IS DEFINITELY NOT AN OPTION

In these stories we have focused on the various tricks our brains can play on us. But what about the rest of our physical body? A critical factor that can play an awful and insidious role in our later lives is obesity. Too many of us, both men and women are overweight. My favourite people, the media, seem to focus their comments and support on people from teenagers to those in their fifties. They seem to have forgotten there are people from fifty and up who are battling this disease, and the needs of these people are more important than those of a youngster.

The ever expanding group of sixty plus, which includes some of the baby boomers, is battling overweight problems compounded by decreasing metabolic rates and increasing problems with mobility. Note that mobility doesn't just encompass exercise; it is everything we do in the way of moving our bodies.

We were given arms and legs and this fantastic organ known as the brain to enable our internal and external body functions; but in order for them to operate, we are meant to move, move, and move. Overweight does not kill outright, but it offers a spiralling downward plunge into the miserable world of disability from which, in our vintage years, we may not recover. We all accept that different diets work for different people, and since we have a myriad of movements (exercise) available, we can choose the one most beneficial to us.

Whether you want to diet or just eat sensibly, **just do it.** Walking, gardening, housework, swimming – it doesn't matter, **just do it** and with regularity. To prove my point, when I had a dog to walk, we walked every morning. Not a huff and puff race walk, but a slow, steady one. When there were no dogs, I put on ten pounds. Worse still, the mobility of one leg ground to a standstill. Ignoring movement and exercise is so easy to do, but ignore it at your peril. I know many of you may rightly argue that I could still have walked without the dog. Would you do it every day in the pouring rain if you had a choice? With a dog, you have no choice.

We need to think seriously about this situation because this is going to affect our quality of life. Weight loss, even just five pounds, will relieve an enormous amount of pressure on our skeletal system. Wouldn't it be great to get those old bones working with greater ease?

Let's do it.

THE DUMPED DUMPLINGS

by Denis Parsons

I have been intrigued with the 'Musings of an Old Biddy'. I don't know what the male equivalent of an old biddy is called, but never mind; we should be allowed to have our say. I have to confess also, there are many times when I feel I'm not quite with it. To prove it, my attempt at cooking a stew the other day was the crème de la crème of stupidity, I am ashamed to confess.

I like to experiment with cooking and recently made a steak and kidney pudding that I used to love as a child in England. However, having gone to town with the ingredients and producing an excellent pudding, there was so much steak and kidney left over, I thought a stew would be nice With my stews I always like to have dumplings, large and fluffy dumplings, so I set about making them. Out came my scales to measure the ingredients for dumplings. I weighed three ounces of shredded suet and put that into a dry pudding basin. Next, I added a pinch of salt and thoroughly mixed the suet and salt together. Then came the all-purpose flour and I measured out six ounces of flour.

During this time, the simmering steak and kidney stew was making me feel hungry and I quickly mixed the contents in the pudding basin with sufficient water to bind the dumplings. This is a bit of a messy palaver; the mixed dough had to be moulded into balls the size of –

well it doesn't matter too much. If you like dumplings you can make them large or small. After boosting the simmering stew to boiling point, I carefully forked my balls of dough into the stew.

After twenty-five minutes of cooking time, I served up my stew with my light-as-a-feather dumplings. Biting into one of them, I nearly broke my teeth! My, oh my, what had happened? The dumplings were just as hard as cannon-balls. Was I going insane and if not, what had gone wrong?

Pondering the whole matter, my eyes roamed around the kitchen and came to rest on the scales. I was mortified. There was the carefully measured flour still on the scales instead of in the dumplings. No wonder they were inedible. Obviously I won't live that down in a hurry!

THE DAY THE SCALES CRASHED

"You lie," I screamed as I stood on the scales after two weeks of near starvation, only to find that the indicator was still at the same figure as last time I weighed myself. In blind fury I jumped with all my might on the scales, and that, I am afraid, was the end of my weighing apparatus.

I was desperate and the problem was – what on earth could I do about it? After all, the medical profession, weight loss companies, and diet pundits trumpet their success mainly with young, nubile women who achieve fantastic weight losses in a record period of time. Not once do you hear about a plodding, older, slower woman who has achieved any kind of success following the same regimen in any period of time, as in my case.

Make no mistake about it, the weight loss organizations will assert if you stick to a diet, preferably their particular diet, then you *will* lose weight. There is no one, I am certain, absolutely no one living who has more experience dieting over the past forty years than I do. Furthermore, I know my body inside out and back to front. Success was always mine when I was younger, even when I thought I was overweight at size fourteen! Now, nothing moves. Not even exercise in a gym for three months four times per week and a diet of approximately fourteen hundred calories can assist.

I sit and chat with doctors who admit "they don't know." I saw a specialist in obesity who was over the moon with the prospect of having another guinea pig for drug-controlled diet tests. When he found out that due to a particular medication I was taking, I didn't fit the specifications of the test drug manufacturer, I was dropped immediately.

What can be done? It seems to be a well-known fact that as you grow older, it becomes much more difficult to lose weight because our metabolic rate starts to slow down. For a person like me who is in possession of a stubborn body, the weight control organizations, while never admitting defeat, give up on you. The medical profession cannot help so they humour you with the admission that they simply don't have any answers except the old maxim that the less calories you consume, the more weight you will lose. This may generally be true, but I think it depends on how different bodies respond to different diets and, of course, the difference in age. An eight hundred calorie diet for me yielded no success because my body thought it was being attacked and went into shut down mode.

The only time I lost weight on a few calories was in a hospital bed for ten days, drinking three meal replacement drinks a day. As for your nearest and dearest friends and relatives, they utter silly platitudes like – get comfortable with your overweight image and accept it and stop worrying about it. Not on your life!

The above arguments are not acceptable for me – not when you are clinically obese and time is running out. It is not a healthy situation viewed in any light. I want to continue life as a fit and healthy woman enjoying a good quality of life, so shedding weight is a must. Growing old with an obesity problem is not an option.

BROKEN DISH OF MEMORIES

This is a sad lesson about being focused on what you are doing when busy and not allowing yourself to think about other things, I was cooking the Sunday lunch a couple of weeks ago, and the roast was in a casserole dish that had been in my family for years and years. There was nothing special about this dish. It was a rather drab brown, rectangular stoneware dish with gently sloping sides about two inches in depth. It was not a particularly attractive dish to look at. It was just there, and it was used for *everything* that was going into the oven. It seemed to be just the right size for all the dishes I cooked, and I rarely used another cooking utensil except for turkeys and large roasts.

During this Sunday lunch preparation, I removed the tin foil lining and picked up the dish to put it in the sink. Because it had been sitting on top of the stove for some time, I thought it would be quite cool and so I didn't bother to put on the oven mitt. It was not cool. It was hot, hot, and hot. It was off the oven top, over the floor and on the way to the sink before I realized my fingers were burning. I dropped it with a shriek of pain. Upon making contact with the floor, my beloved casserole dish broke into a thousand pieces.

My shriek of pain, turned to tears of anger, and then painful tears of anguish because I had lost a piece of family history. Crowded thoughts of many years suddenly appeared in my head, particularly of my parents and two sisters. This dish had reminded me of the love and warmth we enjoyed as a family, together with the heartaches and tears (not too often), which were not enjoyed.

It reminded me of a quieter and much more serene life many years ago – a time when families interacted and entertained themselves instead of relying on television. A time when life was much gentler and certainly less complicated. I suppose I could go on, but what is the point? The casserole dish is no more and neither is my youth. I guess that was the reason for my tears.

ON THE ROAD AGAIN

CAN YOU GET THERE FROM HERE?

by Jean Oliver

I decided it was time my oldest friend Verna, met my "old" friend Ruth. Ruth and Bill lived in a trailer court just south of Edmonton, Alberta. As usual, we had done nothing in the way of planning before we set off, except to get a few directions. I don't know why people give us directions because we never use them!

Once in Vancouver, I suggested we take the road through Port Coquitlam and, Maple Ridge on the other side of the Fraser River, rather than the freeway straight to Hope. We figured the back way would be much less boring than the freeway. It all sounded simple enough and we would avoid a lot of traffic. Dream on! I had lived in Coquitlam for twenty-nine years but who would have thought in the last ten years since we left a whole new city had grown up. So eventually, being women and not men, we did ask for directions and managed to follow enough of them to get us on our way.

We drove off the ferry at about ten o'clock in the morning and should have been well into our journey before supper. As it was, we only arrived at Hope in the late afternoon – a mere seventy-five miles from Vancouver. So much for trying to avoid the freeway.

Getting out of Hope was a little easier than getting out of Vancouver. We only had to ask a service station guy once for directions to the Coquihalla Pass and he just pointed over our shoulder at the large sign that said "This Way." Not in those words, but you know what I mean.

Once over the Coquihalla, we took a secondary highway to avoid Calgary. We were getting close and weren't sure (surprise) which was the road to Bill and Ruth's place. A phone call to Bill and he said, to turn on to such and such a road and follow it to their place and he would meet us at the road into the trailer park. Well, naturally we took the wrong road, got lost, and had to return to the highway.

Following the highway for a short distance, we saw ahead of us about six or eight Royal Canadian Mounted Police officers with three or four police cars. Obviously there was a serious problem for the R.C.M.P. We just pulled into their road block. I mean people are usually pulled over at a road block; you don't go into one! They looked puzzled, like "What the heck are these two old biddies doing?" One officer came over to the car and I asked him if he knew where such and such a road was. He pointed to a matter of yards from where they had set up their road block. Again, there was a nice big sign telling us this was the road we wanted. As we pulled away looking back we could see all these officers scratching their heads and smiling.

We finally made it to Ruth and Bill's place and after a pleasant visit with them for a few days, we took off and made our way to the Yellowhead Highway and Prince George, for Verna to visit her brother and me to visit my sister-in-law. The only unplanned incident we had on the way to Prince George was the matter of gas. We followed one of those signs that say "Gas Ahead." I might suggest to our readers, that when you see a sign that says "Gas Ahead," unless you can actually see the garage, don't go.

I thought at the time we didn't have much choice, but I since realized we probably had enough gas for another one hundred miles. Off we went following the signs along a side road. We seemed to travel for an eternity until we finally saw a house with a sign that said "Gas." There were no pumps in sight, or people, so we drove round the back of the house. A young girl came out and directed us to the one pump. This was Alberta, oil-rich province of Canada, so maybe you're entitled to have your own gas pump!

With a full tank of gas, we left the gas house and instead of turning back the way we came, we just carried on into unknown territory; I don't know why we keep doing this? Again, it was another long journey until we came to a house where a couple were working in their yard. I stopped the car and asked the fellow if he could tell us how to get back on the highway. He went into a lot of turn here, go half a mile, turn left and so on. Finally, frustrated, his wife came over to us and said "Don't listen to him, he will only get you lost. Men don't understand how women think." So she told him to get into the car and lead us back on to the highway, and he did. We really liked that lady.

The rest of the trip was uneventful but funny. However, it involved relatives so we won't go into that; you'll just have to take my word that it was fun.

ARE WE THERE YET?

No matter how well prepared we think we may be for a journey, sometimes we can make a vitally important mistake.

Eileen, Norma, Pat and Betty decided to go to Victoria. The Royal British Columbia Museum had been advertising an exhibit of artefacts from the British Museum, and the girls thought it would be interesting and would make a pleasant day out.

Eileen, who is a very efficient organizer, agreed to take care of reservations for a one- night stay in a hotel. The rest of the girls were quite happy to let her get on with her planning. The only stipulation they made was that the hotel be close to the museum that was in downtown Victoria.

There were three hotels in the area, the Queen Victoria Inn, the Chateau Victoria and the Executive House. However, they were all a little more than the girls wanted to pay. Eileen did note that one of the hotels advertised a price reduction shortly, so she decided to phone later when the lower prices became an option.

The four left Nanaimo early with Betty at the wheel of the car. The drive to Victoria was excellent and about three hours from Nanaimo. They decided en route to get settled at the hotel before going to the museum for the rest of the day.

As they reached the outskirts of Victoria, Betty asked which hotel Eileen had chosen. Eileen thought it was the

Chateau Victoria, but wasn't quite sure, but she would know as soon as she saw it. When the hotel came into view, Eileen decided that the Chateau was definitely not the hotel they were looking for. Putting her hand on Betty's shoulder, she suggested Betty could turn the car around and head for the Queen Victoria Inn.

"Yes, this is our hotel," Eileen said with a sigh of relief as they drove up to the entrance. Everyone got out of the car and followed Eileen to the reservations desk. They relished the idea that within a few minutes they would be off to the museum, which of course was the whole purpose of the trip.

"I'm sorry," said the girl behind the reservations desk looking at the slip of paper Eileen had provided, "but this is not one of our reservation numbers and we have no record of you coming to stay with us tonight." Eileen looked stunned and the girls' faces mirrored her concern. Eileen's mind went into overdrive. Having dismissed the Chateau Victoria when she first saw it, she now thought she *must* have booked there. "Would you be kind enough to telephone the Chateau Victoria," she asked the sympathetic-looking receptionist, "to see if they have a reservation for us?" But even after that telephone call, they were no further ahead. The Chateau Victoria had never heard of them.

Poor Eileen, who is usually the epitome of efficiency, now looked decidedly fussed, and her mind was frantically trying to work out what had happened. Of course, it didn't help that the rest of the girls and the receptionist were trying to offer some helpful hints, even though they didn't have a clue as to how the mix-up occurred.

Frantically trying to sort out the booking procedures she had used back home, a vague notion occurred to her.

What if she had mistaken the telephone numbers on the brochure? She asked the receptionist if the hotel had a copy of the visitor's guide she had used when she did the initial bookings by phone. Ten minutes later the guide surfaced and was almost snatched up by a grateful Eileen.

Turning to where the Queen Victoria Inn was listed, she ran her fingers down the page until she reached the Queen Victoria Inn and then moved across the page. In the next column there was the Quality Inn, and next to it was probably the telephone number she used, thinking it belonged to the Queen Victoria Inn.

A quick call to the Quality Inn confirmed their booking. From that moment onwards, Eileen began to feel considerably better. Of course, it was not as close to the museum as they had wanted it to be, but it was only four blocks farther out and at least they had a bed for the night – at the lower rate. All four of them were beginning to have nightmares that involved sleeping in a tent in the nearby park.

After thanking the receptionist profusely for all her help, the girls departed in the car for the museum, which they enjoyed very much – comforted by the fact that they didn't have to worry any more as to where they were going to sleep.

The following morning, after a comfortable night and a good breakfast, they headed back to Nanaimo, having thoroughly enjoyed their Victorian adventure.

NO TIME TO SMELL THE ROSES

by Jean Oliver

Verna's husband passed away ten plus years ago. Since then, my good friend Verna and I have taken a road trip somewhere every year. Don, my husband, is quite happy for me to go on these trips, just as I am happy to see him go snowboarding in the winter. We do manage to get away together at some time during the year. However, this year I am not so sure because he has the garden to look after.

Back to the trip with Verna. We always take our cameras along for the ride. Halfway through the trip we decide we should take some pictures and we did – just once. For example, I have several pictures of stunted trees in Alberta and Verna has many pictures of sand formations we saw at a rest stop. That is about the extent of our picture taking. Each trip we stop and take pictures of vague, undefined, and boring landscapes somewhere along the way. We don't even take pictures of each other. If we did, we would only look at them and wonder who those two old biddies are.

As you would probably tell us, we should stop and smell the roses on our trips, instead of traveling from A to B in one mad dash to get there. I am also thinking it is about time we traded our cameras in and got a camcorder. I am sure it would make for some interesting dialogue!

I bet we are the only two people who toured the

southern and western half of Vancouver Island in two days! For those of you not familiar with Vancouver Island, that is about four or five days of touring at the pace old biddies generally tour. We planned on taking a week because we have to figure on getting lost, at least once.

The first day we went south to Victoria, and then on to Sooke. The following day we travelled back up the Island again and did the West Coast. Actually, we never got lost once. Confused – yes – but not lost. For instance, friends told us we should go to the Wickaninnish Inn on the West Coast, and have lunch. According to them it was a great place to visit. Well, we went there and didn't think it was *that* hot. In addition, we couldn't find out where our friends had eaten.

Later we discovered there are two Wickaninnish Inns, the old and the new. Of course we went to the old which is now just an information centre and a place from which you can view the Pacific Ocean. Furthermore, the two inns are nowhere near each other.

We drove to Ucluelet approximately thirty kilometres down the road, where we had lunch in an old boat that had become a restaurant. The food was good. After lunch I asked where the rest room was and was directed to the head of some stairs. Ah, life is never that simple for us. Down I went into the bowels of the ship, and at the bottom was a long hallway which I followed, right into what looked like crew quarters. At least there was a bathroom complete with toothbrushes and other grooming gear.

It was eerie and apparently I was the only one down there. I suddenly realized if I yelled for help, nobody would hear me. Also, I was now beginning to doubt myself. This couldn't be the rest room for the restaurant because those stairs were pretty steep and you had to step over a sill from room to room. There was no way it was a wheelchair-friendly place. I worked my way back upstairs to where Verna was beginning to wonder if I had gone for a swim. I suggested to her if she had to use the bathroom, we'd stop at the first garage and she could use theirs.

Did I mention this year we are planning (the only way Verna and I plan is to just get in the car and drive), a trip to the northern most part of the Island?. We will just go till we run out of road. I am planning to pick Verna up at the ferry in Comox. If we are going to get lost, this would be the time, trying to get out of Comox!

I figure this is the only reason why she and I take these jaunts, so we can get together and have a lot of laughs. We laugh at things other people don't think are funny and we learn new words to call all the other drivers on the road.

LOSING IT

DOWN MEMORY LANE

How many of us, I wonder, think that because we take the milk carton to the bathroom, instead of the fridge, we *really* are losing it! Take heart, I offer re-assurance for those of us in that predicament.

About fifteen years ago, I attended a seminar on "Your Memory," in the hope I would find some answers to my forgetfulness at that time, never mind now. In many respects the seminar was just what I expected, but from another angle it was quite outstanding. The particular explanation I heard concerning forgetfulness and memory as we grow older has stayed with me to this day; in my advancing years, it gives me great comfort.

The speaker likened our brain to the hard disc drive of a computer. When we first begin to use the computer, there is a brand-new hard drive which is fast with little data on the drive. The more we use it and the longer we have it, the slower it becomes as we ask the computer to retrieve information from the hard drive. To grant our request, the computer must sort through hundreds and thousands of files and materials now on its hard drive, so it takes a tad longer to get the answer.

So it is with our brain. The older we get, the more difficult it becomes to retrieve and enunciate information from our brain. If it is difficult for a computer to find material in less than one second, imagine the pressure on our brains which hold a life time of data – much more than a small computer can ever hold.

So we mumble or grumble, or to be honest, curse and swear because we can't think of the word we want to use, somebody's name, or even worse, where was that something we put away for safety! Remember, this is all quite normal and not an indication of an underlying serious problem. No, we are not getting senile.

This explanation provided to me by the memory seminar all those years ago, has served me well indeed and I just wanted to pass it along to you as a reminder.

FORGET ME NOT!

Our senior moments are growing, not diminishing, so it would seem. The following is a prime example.

"Come on, supper time," I called to Rufus our dog after giving his food a final stir. I sailed into the dining room and put his bowl on the table. I called again.

"Come on, supper time."

Why was Rufus sitting in the kitchen with a puzzled look on his face?

"Ouch," I said to myself. I picked up the bowl and backtracked to the kitchen, putting the bowl down on his table. No wonder the poor dog looked confused.

On another occasion, I was wrapping up the leftovers to go into the fridge. Where did they end up? In the bathroom. How, oh how, could I be so stupid?.

Really, these senior moments are becoming all too frequent.

It was changing sheets day and I was going to put the set of pink sheets on the bed. Trouble is I couldn't find the pink sheets. They were not in the linen closet and I checked out the linen closet downstairs which revealed nothing. Perhaps I had put them in one of the drawers in the spare bedroom downstairs – remote, but possible. No, they were not there. In desperation I looked into the semi-storage room, just in case. There was no sign of any pink sheets.

I was getting myself worked up about these bed linens. After all, a pair of sheets and pillow cases didn't just walk out of the house. The more I fussed, the worse the situation appeared and finally I asked my husband if he had seen the pink sheets.

"Yes," he said. "They're on the bed."

Apart from these bizarre trivialities that arrive more frequently as we grow older, there are the more delinquent problems that affect our sense of comfort. For example, brandishing that Hollywood smile at a bridge game and then remembering you forgot to put in your partial plate. Not only are you making whistling sounds as you speak through the teeth that are not there, but there is also the most embarrassing black hole in our teeth.

The car keys and our inability to remember where we put them can cause some screaming and swearing, especially when we are in a hurry to go out and they are nowhere to be found and we have an appointment or deadline to meet. Not only that, but there is always the possibility of losing the keys so you can't drive home.

Finally, there are glasses. For most of my life I have been short-sighted and was never able to see much beyond the end of my nose without glasses, which I wore all the time. On becoming bi-focal, I had to wear lenses though which everything appeared to be distorted. It was a nightmare. I finally resorted to wearing two pairs of glasses – one for distance use and the other for reading. That was a nuisance, but it worked.

This last year I had cataracts removed from both eyes. It was such a glorious feeling to see clearly into the far distance again. I felt liberated. I knew before the operation that I would have to wear glasses for reading, but had temporarily forgotten about this on a shopping spree shortly after my last operation. I went to buy some clothes, and no matter how hard I tried to decipher the price and size tag, nothing less than putting the garment on the floor, and then zooming in on it until I could see would suffice. I was very much aware of the odd looks coming in my direction. Many times I forget to take my glasses with me (for reading, that is) and I have to ask a complete stranger to read something for me. How embarrassing can it get?

This incident precipitated a furious round of activity to equip myself with reading glasses to be placed strategically around the house. No glasses on a chain around my neck for me. If anything dates you it is specs on a chain around your neck. I did try, but the glasses either slipped out of the chain holders or I caught the chain on something and it broke.

I now have glasses in the den, kitchen, bedroom, bathroom, lounge, dining room, and handbag. Yet still I walk from room to room carrying or wearing the specs and then leave them in the destination room. When I return to the original room and can't find them, all hell breaks loose and my blood pressure shoots way up high.

So life goes on but does "forget me not," get any better? No, I don't think so. It goes with the territory and we have to devise a plan. I'll let you know when I have one.

HAVE YOU SEEN MY CAR?

The following is something a lot of us have in common, but it is an experience that makes you want the ground to swallow you up!

I stayed with my son, daughter-in-law, and granddaughter, Vera, while in Vancouver, and discovered that Vera had little in the way of books to read. Apparently her books were left in the Philippines because transporting them by air was a no-go due to weight. So, I promised Vera I would buy her some new books when I went out on Monday.

Monday afternoon found me in the children's book department in Chapters, Metrotown, Burnaby. I was in my element among children's books, but unfortunately my legs were causing me problems because of all the work over the weekend and I had to keep sitting down. Sitting down was what I was going to do anyway, because I had arranged to meet my second son and my ex-husband in Metrotown for a chat, but in the meantime I had to find the books.

Of course, the boys were late and very late, so after choosing the books, I decided the best thing for me was to return to downtown Vancouver as it was getting a little late for a meeting. Off I went to get the car and be on my way, but upon arrival at the parking place, there was no car. Round the entrance island I went for a couple of times, getting more panic-stricken because in the trunk of the car was a fair amount of cash I was to give someone downtown. Finally, on legs that would hardly carry me, I made my way to the mall administration office to enquire whether any cars had been towed. No, they had not and it was suggested I see security right away.

Even after their directions to the security office, I couldn't find it. Almost in tears, I made my way back to Chapters to sit for a while. Suddenly, manna from heaven – a security guy appeared walking out of Chapters and I immediately confronted him. Unfortunately, he didn't represent the branch of security I wanted, but he did kindly offer to have a rep from traffic security come to me so I wouldn't have to walk.

The traffic security rep arrived five minutes later, seemingly quite enthused and amused about assisting a doddery old woman who had lost her car. He told me how, quite often, people lost their car in the parkade, because they couldn't remember where they had parked it. I assured him I was always attentive as to where I parked my car in parking lots and parkades, so there was little possibility of me forgetting where I had put the car.

At his request, I gave him all the details, took his duly offered arm, and rode the escalator down to the next floor. We went through the same procedures I had gone through when I came to look for the car, and nothing was to be found. Finally, as we walked back into the building again, he turned and asked me if I had checked the lower level.

Ding- dong! A huge bout of acute embarrassment swept over me because I hadn't even thought about the lower floor. This thought was mixed with the excitement of possibly finding the car and the money. Down to the next level we went and walked to where I had parked the car. As we came out of the building doorway and turned in the direction of the parking spot, I spotted the gleaming bright-red of the hood belonging to my rented car. I nearly jumped for joy.

The security rep couldn't have been nicer in the face of acute embarrassment by yours truly. When we arrived back at Chapters, he even offered to go and find my son who was hopefully looking for me just outside the main entrance of Chapters. When they arrived, I knew by the look on Michael's face that it would be a while before I lived down that experience. I had hoped it would be over and done with that day, but that was not going to happen.

THE FUNKY LAUNDRY ROOM

For the first time I have to admit I can no longer go like a bat out of hell to accomplish certain projects. Like most older people, I feel my mind is still operating at a much younger age. You feel nothing can hold you back from accomplishing whatever you set your mind to do – until you start!

Multitasking has already become a thing of the past and I am quite incapable of thinking about more than one thing at any one time. So, I must admit defeat in the "do it in five minutes department," as far as the funky laundry room was concerned (funky, new Biddy term for messy).

The laundry room in our house is like a bottomless pit for all things having no specific home. How great it is to have a room like this? The advantages are as follows:

You don't have to think where to put something.

You know you can shut the door and forget about whatever you've put in there.

You have the freedom to put the article on the nearest shelf or in any space you can find – even piled on top of other things, if necessary.

You don't have to remember to put it away later.

It is one fewer thing littering the rest of the house.

Yes, the laundry room is the perfect resting place for all things that don't have a designated place – until it is time to clean it up because there is simply no more room for anything else and you can't even get the door closed. This creates some massive problems, not the least of which is a husband who has items stored he hasn't touched for three years! If I tell him about his cache, he will dig his heels in even further. If I throw out anything, he will eventually discover this at some point and the hell that will break loose is not even worth thinking about! He is just too doggone lazy and a pack rat.

The cleaning up of the laundry room, which normally should take one hour, now seems endless. Alas, this is the first admission of being "out to lunch," on planning issues. I fussed around here and there, creating more work for myself because I had no plan. To cut a long story short I spent about 2.5 hours cleaning up before making lunch. After lunch, I spent about half an hour arguing with myself about the whole darn mess, and then gave up. What a waste of time – this arguing with oneself, I mean. The laundry room isn't going to run away – it has been in a complete mess for about six months, so one more day shouldn't matter. Furthermore, even if it isn't finished tomorrow, it will be finished the next day – so what.

The worst is yet to come; I still have to convince one husband that something like the package of deer hair he is hoarding for fly tying for fishing, is not at the top of the list of items to be kept, since he stopped fishing about three years ago!

ABOUT THE AUTHOR

Susan was born in Yorkshire, England and now lives on Vancouver Island, Canada. She had plenty of opportunity to hone her writing skills as a business consultant, but a disabling accident in 1996 turned her life upside down. She could no longer travel in her work, so she decided to finally turn to writing. She has written *Hell's Gate Trilogy* for juveniles, a management book called *The Frog Snogger's Guide* and two booklets on self- help.

Just published is *Stay Young The Golden Years Are The Pits*. Susan has taken her experience and humour to write a funny/serious book about growing old.

HELL'S GATE TRILOGY

These juvenile fantasy novels are powerful and exciting. Kate, James and Amanda, along with Kate's guardian angel, Oscar, the ostrich, become accidentally involved in three dangerous adventures in different countries. Along for the ride are Jenza, the Siberian Tiger and Isia, the bald eagle, very old angel friends of Oscar, to ensure that the children are kept from real harm.

The Diamond Talisman: in Wales, U.K. at the Marquess of Ryerdale's Estate. The friends are helping the Marquess search for the fabulous and priceless Mirendah Diamond which originated in the Middle East. Unfortunately, they are not the only ones searching for the Diamond; the notorious Corr Gang wants it too – and they will do anything to get this very old and extremely valuable gem.

The Caves & The Skull: in the Bahamas where the mysterious Island of Doge beckons the teens. They have no idea that Doge is the headquarters of Mr. X and that the local police services, assisting the Secret Service of the United States, have been trying to find Mr. X for a very long time, together with his international ring of gangsters and smugglers. The trouble is, Mr. X does not want to be found by anyone.

Hell's Gate: in British Columbia, Canada where Hell's Gate, part of the mighty Fraser River, is a gold digger's paradise in 1858! Read how the youngsters journey back in time to 1858 to deal with Rotgut Joe and his ruffians who would rather steal mining claims than dig for gold.

Suitable for a reading age of 9+ with no profanity. There are also subtle suggestions of Christian values for young readers.

To order a copy or copies of Hell's Gate please contact Snosrap Publishing at: *http://snosrappublishing.com* or contact us at *sanden39@shaw.ca*